In this house are many women

In this house are many women

SHEREE FITCH

GOOSE LANE

Published with the assistance of the New Brunswick Department of Municipalities, Culture and Housing and the Canada Council, 1993.

Cover painting: #6 from the series "Women" (detail), by Jacqueline Riemer,1992, egg tempera and ink on gessoed paper mounted on rag. Book design by Julie Scriver.
Printed in Canada by The Tribune Press.
10   9   8   7   6   5   4

Canadian Cataloguing in Publication Data

Fitch, Sheree
    In this house are many women

    Poems.
    ISBN 0-86492-164-0

I. Title.

PS8561.I8616 1993   C811'.54   C93-098643-1
PR9199.3.F57I6 1993

Goose Lane Editions
469 King Street
Fredericton, New Brunswick
Canada E3B 1E5

In my life are many women
and this book is for them
and from them and is dedicated
to the memory of my
mother's mother
Alberta Doucet Comeau

Acknowledgements

Much of this material was written or reworked in 1988 with the support of a Canada Council Arts Grant "B."

Special thanks to Kathy Allison, for original retyping; and to Mary Danckert, for her gift of the word Propinquity, which she gave to Paula who gave it to me.

Some of these poems have appeared in *The Fiddlehead* and *Alpha* and have been broadcast on "Morningside," "Atlantic Airwaves," "Cloud Nine," "Some Assembly Required," "Main Street," "Maritime Noon," and various other CBC radio programs.

Contents

In this house are many women

The Runner   *13*

Exit   *17*

Marie Leads the Way   *19*

What Rhoda Remembers About
    the First Five Minutes   *21*

Filling Out The Form   *23*

Edna   *24*

Jane's Observation Notes   *26*

Charlotte's First Night   *27*

Barbara   *30*

Edna Remembers Exactly How It Goes   *32*

Valerie Listens to Gwendolyn   *34*

Helen's List   *36*

The Fashion Show   *37*

If I do say so myself   *40*

Neighbour   *42*

Marie's Lullaby   *43*

Propinquity

Grand-mère   47
Mother to Infant   50
Villa Madonna   51
In the Still Dark   55
Flannelism   56
Garbage Man   57
Hero   59
Coming of Age   61
Advice   62
Madonna   64
Cop   66
Civil Servant   69
Grand LaPierre, Newfoundland
    (for Ross Elliott)   73

Ever-spinning cupid

Puzzle   79
Shopping with a Friend for her Wedding
    Dress   81
Overheard Tale   82
When Flesh Suggests   84
Lucy in Parts
    The Love Song of Lucy Lament   86
    Lucy On Married Men   88

Lucy On Monogamy   *89*

Lucy On Marriage   *90*

Lucy On Younger Men   *91*

Lucy's Warning   *93*

Lucy and the Window Washer   *94*

Lucy On BUTS   *95*

Random Moments   *96*

Ever-Spinning Cupid   *98*

Diana's circus

Interior Decorating   *103*

Monday   *105*

Tuesday   *107*

Wednesday   *111*

Thursday   *113*

Friday   *114*

Saturday   *116*

Sunday   *117*

Night Shift   *118*

Postscript   *119*

In this house are many women

The Runner

She runs:

> past men in blue suits with red ties
> men bunched by the elevator door
> men in denim jackets and jeans
> huddled by a cigarette machine

She runs:

> past women with drawstring mouths
> women with wombs puckered out
> from plum to grape to raisin
> women who have never known
> what wetness means

She runs: in this outer space and finds a door

She rests:

> a drummer sidesteps up to her
> whispers in her ear
> *I'd like to get to know you*
> *yesIwouldindeedIwouldIreallywould*

She runs:

        in fear of the lion

She rests
She watchs

She appeals to a lady
beneath a red and white canopy
        — what kind of place is this
        and what day

but the lady snaps shut her compact
does an about turn high heel walk away
on her back is a piece of cardboard
cut with pinking shears
words in green felt tip marker

She reads:
        I AM APHRODITE

So she runs:

        past a candy counter of green and gold and red foil
        through glass doors marked pull
        past a barbershop
        through a parking lot
        to Brunswick street
        where she stops before a tree

she tries to embrace this tree
this tree with bark
that is grey and green not brown
but the trunk is too thick
she cannot reach her arms around
and clasp her hands

A voice yells:

> *hey lady why are you hugging that tree for?*

So she climbs:

> (to make it look like she has business there)

but the first branch is too high
she cannot find a toehold
the man who lives on the top branch
spits on her saying:

> *— it's already been sold*
> *this is my tree*
> *go find your own*

She runs
She runs
She runs
She sniffs the sound of a telephone ringing
far in the distance
She follows the sound
She finds the phone

The voice on the other end rasps:
— *is this the RCMP?*

She runs

becomes the woman wailing beneath
the weeping willow tree
rapunzel rapunzel letting down her long hair

gets up and walks in slow motion sliding image
dissolves to X to X to Exit

Exit

when in danger one must
exit to the left:
in one peculiar gesture
a straddling

                 side-step

among
the marigolds

proceed beyond lunar
boundaries
wrapped in

                 moonlight

swaddling

among the nightingales
there is no tomorrow

the secret lies
in perspicacity

in capacity
or rose petal down

                 yodel from that distant peak

in glacial tones

swoop to mirror magic

listen to
bird bones

rattling

Marie Leads the Way

Take any street in midday heat in any city or town
on an August afternoon
sit down on a bench beneath a maple tree
watch the women and you'll see
high heels and denim jeans
hair pulled back in twisted knots
or freely falling raven locks
young girls with ribbons in their tresses
patent leather shoes and frilly dresses
teens with breasts so firm and full and giggles high
spilling out the secrets they are finding out
women wearing pantyhose and skirts with slits
satin shirts almost like designer ones
in trendy magazines where all the women
are long and lean
listen as they walk staccato on the sidewalk
upright paper cut-out dolls marching
marching marching
then the baggy saggy trundling women
weary of the burdens and the bundles
in their arms
tired of giving
tired of living
but trekking on trucking on

in their eyes all the edges
of the many stories of survival
see this one here is in the midst
of such a story
see how her shoulders hunch
how her step is like she's testing
out the street as if it's made
of quicksand quick get up
follow her
travel past the shopping malls and restaurants
down a narrow residential street
where you pass by windows get a glimpse
of photographs in gilded frames
on wooden tables
see how so many people hang their family pictures
over mantels
follow her until you come to *the house*
one house that looks the same
as all the others but is not
this house is a womb
of many rooms
in this house
are many women

What Rhoda Remembers About the First Five Minutes

pressing the buzzer
thinking how ugly
the sound of a buzzer

an intercom voice asking: who is there
wanting to say me just me
choking on my name

the sound of my voice
thinking how ugly
the sound of my voice
making
it all too real

doors unlocking
the woman named Valerie
her eyes like pillows
a calico cat on a green paisley couch
a desk piled high with papers

then there were whispers
a kind of chorus:

> someone new is coming
> someone new is coming
> someone new is coming
> do we have enough room
> someone new is coming
> hear how hard she's crying
> she has a little baby

Valerie's voice apologetic:

> can you please fill out this form?

Filling Out The Form

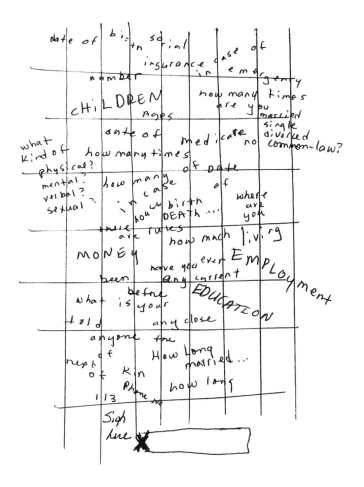

Edna

I   stop
   cannot   the skipping rope voices
    they   come to me
          at the damndest
times like this morning
        I got up while the others were sleeping
started cleaning the kitchen floor
     my mother always said when in trouble
scrub the floor
     that's when they started

     all in together girls
     just fine weather girls

and
this is the way we scrub the floor scrub the floor scrub the
floor
early monday morning
all the way through to
this is the way we go to church go to church go to . . .

garbled voices
                    dripping slowly in my head
a 45 being played at a 33 speed
                    I remember the days of forty-fives
remember today
                    I turn forty-five
as I look in the mirror
                    at my swollen face
wishing I could see
                    the wrinkles

Jane's Observation Notes

3 arrivals
one departure — returned home
see log book for further details

P.S. we need orange juice for tomorrow morning

Came home depressed. John tried to be interested but he was busy working on his thesis. Jennifer left tonight. Went home. Went back. Again. I am not allowed to give advice. Cannot scream don't go. Cannot say I am afraid he will kill you the next time. Just watch her go. Help her with her bags. Hug her kids. Team meeting tomorrow. I need to tell them I need a vacation.

Can't sleep. Tonight I realized when they first come in they all do the same thing. They cannot hold their heads up straight or look me in the eye. They shred a Kleenex or twist it. But what bothers me most is the way they look at the bare wall behind me as if they are studying an abstract painting. As if they are saying there is meaning in there somewhere isn't there, in that wall, there must be, if only I could tilt my head the right way, maybe I would get it.

Charlotte's First Night

everyone is sleeping
the house is breathing
a clock is ticking
it is hot
too hot
the room
smells
like a hospital
Lysol and Mr. Clean
like someone has scrubbed
and rubbed to get
out the germs
the baby is sleeping
in a wooden crib
the bars make a pattern
across her small body
I wear a pink quilted
polyester housecoat
take your pick they
said holding out green
garbage bags
they are old but clean
underneath my window two people
are laughing

that is the strangest thing of all
that out there people are just doing things
like walking and laughing and I am up here
what would they do if they looked up and saw me
standing at a window with bars
who was the woman who washed
and folded this housecoat
and brought it here for me to wear
were her fingernails filed
does she have matching curtains and bedspreads
did she like sex
probably not if she wore a housecoat like this
does she put her hands in the guck
in the kitchen sink at night
when she does the dishes
or does she wear yellow rubber gloves
I know I would hate her if I met her
hate her for having the life
I wanted to have
but tonight I love her
love her for this pink quilted housecoat
for putting it in her green garbage bag
and bringing it here
and who was here before me
and who will wear it after
and what is he doing?

I see him clearly
like me lying in the dark
staring at the wall where
the blinds make a cage of shadows
he is missing me
I know he is
the bed is empty without me there
he knows now he's done it
knows now I am never going back
he is crying I can hear him
crying making that awful sound
the way men cry
the sound of some animal
a wolf maybe
caught in a trap

Barbara

Emily.
she is six
she has a sense of humour
draws pictures of dragons
her eyes are like a rabbit's
pink-rimmed and steady
today I
read her a story
saw a smile
she said she liked
the way the story ended
happy ever after.

Jason. Twelve.
a volcano
today he pounded
a castle his sister
made of play-dough
pounded so hard
he made his knuckles
bleed
called me a bitch
when I told him to stop

my name is Barbara
I said
he pounded the table again
kicked his mother
kicking is not allowed
in this house
I told him
his mother slapped him
slapping is not allowed
in this house
I told her
she said who do you think you are
my name is Barbara
I told her
hitting and name-calling
not allowed
house rules
they both looked
relieved

Edna Remembers Exactly How It Goes

hey mickey and susie were up in a tree they were
doing the
k-i-s-s-i-n-g-thing
next thing you know
was the wedding bell ringing
and people were singing and ever-y-thing
and waah came the baby
and farmer in the dell
well mickey and susie weren't doing very well
singing ashes ashes
wishes in the well
promises are falling down falling down all
the way to
hell

Little Boy Blue has to pay the bills
Little Miss Muffet's on Valium pills

so mickey said to susie
want to go back to that tree
to the time when we kissed
and the kisses were free

but no king's horses
no king's men
could put those two
back together again

mickey and susie
up in a tree
but when the bough breaks
the cradle falls
down comes everyone
baby and all

Valerie Listens to Gwendolyn

Even the many syllables of her name
would indicate she must be the wife
of a man with money
she fingers the gold chains
around her throat
twists her wedding ring
up to her knuckle
as if to let
the white skin underneath
breathe
she has been silent
listening to the others
until:

He has never laid a hand on me
never pushed shoved slapped
I don't have bruises
like the ones you have
mine are invisible
imagine when you look at me
fingermarks like inkstains
underneath my skin
he kept telling me
he wouldn't cheat on me

but he did
again and again and again

I did not leave because of his violence
I left because of mine
I got another phone call
from another woman
I went in and watched him sleeping
saliva like dried chalk
made a rim around his open
mouth
a perfect target

I had a gun
I placed it on his pillow
then I left.

In her suitcase
Gwendolyn has packed
a novel
a flannel nightgown
Oil of Olay
her black silk blouse
because appearance
is important
especially
when you have disappeared

Helen's List

~~Things~~ to do tomorrow:

- get pampers
- phone social services
- tell my mother
- find job
- buy tampax
- peace bond

The Fashion Show

In the kitchen
a fashion show is going on
Rhoda has a job interview
tomorrow morning
so they haul over
the clothing bank donations
as if they are in the
bargain basement
or Frenchy's
they all take turns
see what fits
what her colours are
dress Rhoda up
then Janet
says let me do your hair
Kathy says I'll do the make-up
Rhoda
Rhoda whose stomach bulges
as if she is five months
pregnant
Rhoda who can work wonders
with ketchup and brown sugar
and Kraft Dinner
Rhoda whose skin is sallow

whose hair has been
tangled since she first came in
Rhoda who draws pictures
with butterflies in them
stands up
    metamorphosis
is a buxom
beauty and for just a minute
you believe her when she says
I used to be a looker
a real looker
but who would want
to look at me now.

There is before and after
and then a before
and an after
again
Rhoda whose voice
is filled with thistles
speaks softly
well sir my qualifications are
fuck all
squeals of laughter
then they do like most other nights

make popcorn smoke cigarettes watch television
gather at the table once again
tell their horror stories
sometimes
holding each other

If I do say so myself

farewell
to
welfare

got the job
even got a uniform
how's it look
minimum wage
stickinlickinchicken
the hat's godawful
gotta bobby pin
the dress a bit tight
the stripes are crooked
jeez I look like an
inflatable crooked candy cane

soon I'll have enough
for a down payment
on a mobile home

let me practise
excuse me sir
did you say you wanted
the snack pack party pack

or barrel size
of chicken
that is
have a nice day

then I'll get my
upgrading
maybe take up
guitar again

I used to love
to sing
I've got
a pretty
decent
voice

Neighbour

I will write my Member of Parliament
I will not tolerate this house
in my neighbourhood
it was a nice neighbourhood
before but
last night I saw a shady-looking
character watching
from a car
smoking
drinking beer
I know he was a husband or a boyfriend
of one of those women
I won't have this in my neighbourhood
no I'm afraid I don't have much sympathy
these women bring it on themselves
what's wrong with them
I'd leave the minute any man
raised his hand
where would I go? . . . a friend's I suppose
well, everybody has friends
look maybe it is a good thing
just not in my neighbourhood.
I'm going to write
my Member of Parliament

Marie's Lullaby

I am the angel of this house
house of broken dreams
house where dreams begin again
house of women

At night when you are sleeping
I sing lullabies
lullabies for every Edna
Kathy
Barbara
Helen
Rhoda
Emily
Charlotte
Jane
Gwendolyn
and all the women before you
and all the ones whose names
I do not know yet
who will come after

I sing lullabies for Jason
and all the sons of violence
lullabies for the men who live here

in the nightmares and the dreams
of all the women
hope my song will float and settle
upon their foreheads
like a cool cloth to soothe
the pain fists and words
have caused

I sing lullabies for all the others
living in a house
where there is no shelter

I cradle pain within my wings
sing one more lullaby
pray that someday
in this house of many women
there will not be
any women

Propinquity

Grand-mère

My voice gets lost
in the choke of leaves
coughing down sepia streets

I want to kick the ground
or dig this vacant lot
find a fossil

can you hear me?
                    are you here?

I half expect Christ
to emerge in miniature
on a plastic cross

but there is nothing to be found

only the dandelions growing
from this swollen mound of earth
this whale belly earth
that breathes

whatever happened to Virgin Mary?
Mary, who hung above the kitchen sink

Lady of chipped porcelain
Lady of torn linoleum

Grand-mère

I want your nimble fingers
kneading the knots of your rosary

I need your kiss
on the nape of my neck
your bread-dough arms
your brown sugar whisper

jolie poupée   jolie poupée

I think of you often
pregnant nineteen times

twelve babies twelve kids

I still see your shoes
stretched to fit your feet
swollen purple with veins that burst
in childbirth

Did Mary, ever, just once
see the skin of your torn burlap knees

watch the scrubbing of back porch steps
plead: have mercy?

Did she see the smocking in the camisoles
made from flour sacks
stitched for five daughters

Melvina Lorette Stella Dolores Yvonne

Where was Mary the night
a black New Brunswick highway
killed Gary?

Gary my playmate
Gary your youngest son
Gary your miraculous conception
at forty-seven?

this is no vacant lot

                — you are still here

places left empty have faces
this belly of emptiness so swollen
I ache for a woman
who swallowed the moon

Mother to Infant

this sunshine in my life this warm growing living breathing
bubblebursting filling swelling within   mine own sweet
beautiful baby   lovethisislove   meaning the world the
universe is singing lullabies   flesh of my flesh drink drink
breasts aching heart breaking   the rhythm of your baby's
mouth suctioned at my nipple: tug tug rest   tug tug rest
small coos of satisfaction tug tug rest   sweet streams down
chest milk warm yellow slides down sides of feathercheeks:
sleep baby sleep sleep baby sleep sleepbabysleep

Villa Madonna

There was this woman
in the last pew
in the chapel
at Villa Madonna
that Sunday

It was raining
I couldn't help but think
the drops against the pane
were her tears

grey Sunday
red candle burning
the sisters
brides of Christ
were praying for lost souls
the priest spoke of shadows and valleys
how eyes that looked from windows
could not pass judgement
then:
not worthy so much as to gather up the crumbs
under the table o merciful lord

sisters:
can you pray for me as well
can you take away this ache
can you tell me if my dead child's soul
has made it back to heaven
was it a girl or boy
sisters of charity
shall I name her
find a place in the woods
under a tree
and bury her

it has been so long sisters
sometimes I dream
I wander through a house
hearing the babies crying
but I cannot find them
they are in pain
but I cannot save them
my breasts get heavy and warm
with milk
but still I cannot find them
I wake up and it has rained
on my pillow on my face

I watched her lift the chalice
to her lips
drink the blood

saw arms around her
heard the smothered gurgles
of her womb.

all of that
the whispers of the sisters
the rain
the searing sound
of that woman's pain
the crying of babies
in an old deserted house
comes back to me

but so does the moment
when I saw her shoulders slump
in surrender
and knew she would find rest

how many of us
bring flowers
to the graves
of the children
we never buried
how many of us
have split ourselves
in two
as we watch ourselves

live through a moment
or a nightmare
split ourselves
because if we didn't
we would drown
right there
sitting right there
in a chapel
named after the woman
who also had to witness
the death of her child

In the Still Dark

both my children sleep
I know the rhythm
of their breathing
textures of their skin
the way they are curled in dreams

one moans
the other stirs

I know exactly who does what

I am thankful that in darkness
there are things I know

for tomorrow
when sunlight trembles
through that window there
and eyes ask questions
I would rather not answer

I will not even be sure
of my own voice

Flannelism

At five my son presented me
with a picture of a man in a cowboy hat,
bright red shirt and jeans.

"This is God," he said.
"But Mom his shirt is flannel,
that is important."

I put the picture on the refrigerator.

I have been a Flannelist ever since.

Garbage Man

on Thursdays we hear the crunch of garbage truck
run to watch the garbage man working
underneath the sun
he is young and tanned and wears no shirt
just cut-off jeans
his hair is honey blond
beneath a red scarf turban
a medallion on a chain
dances on his chest
as he builds up his momentum

orangutang swinging from truck to curb
half-running half-leaping
with a rhythm that suggests
he is keeping time to music

the sun shining down on his shoulders
sweat-slippery biceps bulging
hamstrings hard as hammers
pirouetting pirate
in an innovative free-style
garbage day ballet

we call the garbage man
Barishnikov
I tell my children
watch him and remember
when
you do the thing you do with joy
you create a thing of beauty
this is the challenge and the task
of being human:
to take all life's garbage
transform it into dance

I bore them with my metaphor
and my children always wary
of my vision from my window
think he's just a man
in a hurry
to get home for a beer

Hero

"We are going to the jungle"
my father and my son inform me

"Be careful of the lions"
I tell them

My son ties a red terrycloth
superman cape around his neck
my father takes a walking stick
dog on leash
the trio
set off on safari

They are gone many days and nights
or so it seems
for I do worry about the lions
when my cubs have wandered off without me

No need to worry
here they come now

My father is wearing the superman cape
pretending to fly through the neighbourhood
shouting: superman! superman!

My son is running by his side
the dog is yapping
my father in fluorescent red
is making a spectacle of himself

I can see that to my son
this is not a game
of just pretend

My father scoops him up

I watch as they lift into the air
And fly the rest of the way home

Coming of Age

My son is in the bathroom shaving
the water runs. I hear the scrape
across his upper lip, the rinse, the tap
three times on the side of the sink
which makes me wonder if this is some
primordial or innate rhythm all men
are born to repeat this razor tapping
male music ritual.

I wonder this of course
so I won't stop to wonder
how it is this child of mine
grew this hair upon his face
it wasn't much a newspaper smudge
of a mustache
but he told me it was time

It is time
that I am weeping for
how once this child
whose every body part was mine
to clean and tend to
is now a young man
who locks the bathroom door

Advice

Read everything Gloria Steinem ever wrote
her last book first

Ego is like a hat
useful protection
but it should always be taken off
before entering a room
or sitting at a table
with others

You are not only what you do
or who you love
but you must do to discover
who you are
love to discover
why you are

If you're very lucky
you'll get seven minutes of ecstasy
twenty minutes of happiness
so quest after self-knowledge
and inner peace

Finding your balance
is a lifetime
high wire
journey

Keep asking
who is God

Listen to the chorus within
that sings the way
to what comes next

You can always change your mind

The best answers will always be questions

You can always call your aunt

Madonna

real madonnas
are not bullet-breasted singers
making videos and imitating
Marilyn Monroe.

they are women who take care
of other women's children
women who
wipe noses
change diapers
make meals
help children learn
to climb the jungle gym
while their mothers
climb corporate ladders
in stockings and three piece suits
argue court cases
or make minimum wage
which pays rent
and daycare

if I could
I would paint a fresco
of a woman with a rope
around her waist

a rag-taggle of children
following along through the park

her nose would be smudged
with finger paint
her jeans splattered
with playdough

in one hand
I would paint
one half of the university diploma
I studied for
in her other hand
would be the hand
of my child

there would be a halo
around her head

if I sold this painting
I would take her to
a Greek island
where someone could take care of her
where there are no children saying
can I could you I want my Mommie

I would call this painting
Shirley in the Park with the Children.

Cop

Undercover prostitute,
she walked Toronto streets
where she learned the difference
between psychopathic and pathetic
that vanilla
mixed with brown paper
stirred with rain
was the stench of loneliness
that eyes filled with a film of glue
could spill down upon spit-polished boot tips
that tears could come in the midst of city scum.

She found three children
crouched behind a couch
in fear of drunken fists
in the midst of shards of blinking lights
where the tree had crashed down upon
an almost normal family's Christmas Eve.

Another time, she was the first
arriving at a crime
where a ten-year-old
abducted on her way to school
lay bleeding in a ditch

later, at the hospital
tried to give the mother
some reason why
and this was back home
in the Maritimes.

She does all the usual stuff as well
gives out parking tickets, speeding warnings
locks up the city drunks especially in the winter

Days off, she works with power saw
clears the brush from land she bought
fishes there for trout
rides her horse
as she dreams about the home
she'll build
so for a while forgets
the world she walks in.

When she was my kid sister
she was told a girl could not be a cop
but my sister never let
a little thing
like "no such thing"
make her stop.

Today she visits
gun on hip
I meet her
pen in hand

Sisters:
we will the wor(l)d away
in ways that we know how
hold on to hope
as best we can.

Civil Servant

Can I help you?
Can I have your s.i.n.?
113-176-630?
thank you.
next
can I have your sin?
114-456-387?
please have a seat sir
a counsellor will be with you
momentarily

I feel like St. Peter
working front desk
at the UIC office
some have memorized their sins
others fumble
in zippered compartments
put their glasses on
squint
read their sins slowly
as if they can't quite
make them out
then they sit and stare
at walls or scuffed boot tips
the bulletin board or me

I know the regulars
by name and sometimes
delight them
because I know their sins
by heart

every day I sharpen
HB pencils
my daggers
in case anyone should threaten me
people without jobs
get desperate

sometimes I imagine
the battle with pencil and paper and pen
staple gun

when it is over
the floor is stained
with ink drawn directly
from the veins of sin-filled civilians
and the civil servants
whose job it is
to smile while
we tell lies like

it will only be a little while
then someone will take care of you

there was the time a man
threw his record of employment
across the desk at me
all I really remember
was the dandruff
hailstone-size
on his navy blue sweater

another time I was told
there were no groceries
Christmas was the next week
I tried to console
got spit on

what the fuck do you know
stupid bitch you got a job

one time I was given
a bouquet of geraniums
picked from the flower boxes
in front of city hall
because

you work hard
you make me feel okay
when I come in here

waiting rooms make people tired
tired people live in waiting rooms
that is what I learn in this job
daily I am reminded of regional
despair-ity
hear too many confessions
no power to give absolution
or even a bit of hope that someday
the phone will ring
the job they have been waiting for
is theirs

I quit
the guilt
of my conspiracy
dissolved
almost

some nights still
I wake up
having dreamt
people swivel by my desk
in turnstile fashion
my voice is a recorded message

Can I have your sin?
Can I have your sin?

Grand LaPierre, Newfoundland
(for Ross Elliott)

In the Burin in April
one thinks of the word barren

grey against grey

the hills are stubbled with whiskers
with quills
humped backs
of giant porcupines
outlined against an ice-blue sky

the snow is plastic trying to melt
the colour of scorched marshmallow
the grass is dead
the colour is nicotine

the road to the schoolhouse is long

we round the corner and suddenly
there is a live world
houses like children's building blocks
staggered on a hill
multi-coloured stairsteps
leading to a wharf

the mountains like parentheses
on either side
are hugging all these lives within

the ocean, cobalt blue and on and out
as far as I dare look without weeping

I have arrived I think
to that spot on the edge.

The children and teachers
are awaiting my arrival
the halls are decked with pictures:
      lemon tempera sun and tempera green grass

the laughter of these children
sounds to me like the laughter
of balloons

unspoiled children
ready to ask, and touch and hear:

As we twist our tongues around syllables
I try to explain to them
that poetry is everywhere
the wash of waves
the crackle of fire
that no it doesn't have to rhyme
but it must always have a beat

a finger-snap
a toe-tap
that to write one must see and taste and smell and hear and feel
and more than that, must feel the taste must smell the hear

they seem to understand

At noon when they go home
I walk down to the wharf
needing solitude certainly
but more than that, I have an overwhelming
urge to put my finger in the April ocean
to test the temperature of the sea

As I sit here looking out
I am convinced
that no one
in the world is as lucky
as I am at this moment

I turn to head back up

There they are: the children of the morning
streaming down the hill towards me
small children carrying smaller children
shifting babies in woolen bonnets from hip to hip
holding the mittened hands of toddlers

They reach me, they beseech me to do
a reading for their siblings right there
on that wharf, right there on the edge of the Atlantic
then they tell me stories of their fathers at sea
tell me of storms and new bikes they want to buy
and point out where they live

I leave the village
travel to St. John's
that night I dream in tempera technicolour
of a poet named pied piper
who was carried off by children
to a village by the sea

Ever-spinning cupid

Puzzle

When I turned to look at you that morning
I discovered your face
        had arranged itself

in   jigsaw pieces

upon   your   p i ll   ow

your lips had fallen to the floor

there, I thought, lies Orpheus.

What have I done to you, finally?

        Slowly, with early morning fingers

I tried to

        piece you back together

but I could not find the edges

looked into your ear
got lost in the labyrinth

                            all colours blurred

I realized then I must get up and leave you

disassembled   in your box.

Shopping with a Friend for her Wedding Dress

The saleslady
has a nettle
of straight pins in her mouth
and a tape measure necklace

She smiles a porcupine smile

Precisely, she hems the dress
meticulous
about the distance from the hem
to the tips of the *peau de soie* toes

There are rows
of dresses
swathed in plastic
the soft plastic
my mother warned me never to put over my head
because I could suffocate that way
could die that way

Overheard Tale

Sheila Wellington
is back with her lover again
after a six-week reunion
with her husband and kids

her sister says they:

"just can't
figure out
what's come over her
come over her
walking out like that
in the middle of the night
into the arms of an alcoholic
good-for-nuthin and Harold poor Harold
the sweetest
kindest
hardest-working man
you'd ever want to"

"guess she could only
take so much
goodness
would rather live in some

godforsaken hole
in East Saint John
smoke toke drink and screw
her miserable brains out"

"she'll pay   God knows
she'll pay for this
lust only lasts so long
and who'll be there
to pick up her soul and body"

"not Harold not next time"

Sheila Wellington
is back with her lover again
her husband Harold's got the kids

or so her sister says

When Flesh Suggests

My breast falls out of my flannel nightgown
I look at it
as if it is a creature — living
but removed from me

Why look there is my breast!

when was the last time I was touched
or kissed

the voice of my breast
almost inaudible

I thought I'd learned to live
without caress of breasts

I pull the flannel quickly
back across my flesh
to cover up
the moment
but the flannel brushes soft
against my nipple

my skin is hungry

there is nothing I can do
but write a poem

after dancing
it's the next best thing
to making love

Lucy in Parts

The Love Song of Lucy Lament

Shall I wear mascara?
Should I shave my legs?
Will I allow a man
to fertilize my eggs?

Should I take a briefcase?
Should I take a purse?
Will I be a doctor?
Shall I compose a verse?

Should I go to London?
Might I go to Rome?
Shall I do my fingernails?
Should I buy a home?

Will I find good day-care?
Can I afford the rent?
I just received a welfare cheque
I don't know where it went . . .

Will I have a baby?
Shall I take the pill?
Can I, should I, shall I, may I
Might I, won't I, WILL?

Will I scream in labour?
Will my milk come in?
Will I do things right?
Will I have stretch marks in my skin?

Shall I take up biking?
Should I lose some weight?
Should I take a lover?
Or might I meditate?

Shall I run for office?
Will I cut my hair?
Ought I march to Ottawa
in frilly underwear?

Should I buy some fish for dinner?
Shall we eat by candlelight?
Should I take karate lessons?
Will I be safe outside tonight?

Lucy On Married Men

Married men who want to cheat
Usually have this line
"My wife and I have this agreement . . . "
So you nod, then he takes no time
"So I guess we'll go to your place then . . .
Well, we couldn't go to mine."

Or he might just say
"You're incredible" or
"You really turn me on"
The best response to this
Is to look at him and yawn
Take his hand off your thigh
Soak him with your gin
Look him in the eye
And say
"Why sir, adultery's a sin!"

He'll say he loves his wife and kids
He's in a rut and stuck
Walk away, politely say
Sir, I don't give a
session in marriage counselling

Lucy On Monogamy

I've concluded that monogamy
Is like some ancient rare disease
Against which most of us
Have developed immunities . . .

At any rate
It's not a natural state
But for me,
Neither is
Celibacy.

Personally,
I'm into sublimation
I read or write
To fulfill my need
For stimulation

When it gets too difficult
When my blood starts flowing
I scrub out the tub
And listen
To some tunes
By Leonard Cohen

Lucy On Marriage

I'm addicted to intensity
don't want familiarity
want freedom
want adventure
not cooking up baloney
I need
autonomy
instead of
matrimony

Marriage can be
a good thing
It's just not good
for me
I need my independence
Not domesticity

Atleastthat'showIfeelmostofthetimeexceptforlikethismorning
therewasthiscouplestandingintheraintogetherandgettingreadyto
dotheirsaturdaymorningshoppingandtheywerekissingandiwas
wonderingifintensitypermanentlywaspossiblesoallrightsometimes
igetconfusedaboutthisokay

Lucy On Younger Men

I met a young man
At the shopping mall today
He looked at me
In his brown-eyed way
When I turned to go
I heard him say
I want an older woman
Some bad
Someday

He said: You could give me lessons
I said: Yes, I could show you much
He said: I'd really love to learn
I said: I'd show you where to touch
But dear, I do have a confession
I'm not a teacher by profession
Besides an older woman
Wants a man to know
Exactly how fast or slow to go

Yes, an older woman
Wants an older man
Who can
I want a man
Who already can

Well he stood there so dejected
I said: You haven't been rejected
Women have been known to change their minds
Who knows perhaps one day
I will look for you and say
Today, I want a younger man who can
And can and can and can and can!

Lucy's Warning

Beware the tight-lipped
　　　　heavy-lidded man
with zip-locked baggage
he's a vacuum-sealed coffee can

He needs your lips
　　　your fingertips

And you'll become:

a can-opener

to a man
who needs
his mum

Lucy and the Window Washer

A little to the left
no, the right
up a little
down a little
to the left
the left the left
harder slower
higher lower
harder
not that hard
you just missed
the spot

never mind
I'll do it myself

I'm a feminist **BUT** I still really like men it's just the patriarchal white male power structure I don't believe in you understand **BUT** then again maybe I'm not a real feminist with a capital F because I do like lingerie **BUT** I do believe in equality I mean it's really okay for a man to wear lingerie too if he wants **BUT** I believe women just don't have the same privileges as men **BUT** I'm not angry or bitter or lesbian **BUT** what if I was **BUT** I'm not **BUT** I can still be a heterosexual and be a feminist **BUT** I just don't like labels or group mentality anyhow **BUT** maybe you could call me an underdogmatist get it like in underneath the dogma of any ideological stance **BUT** I think just by being here on this planet we're all underdogs anyhow **BUT** I'm not going to say I'm a human being first a woman second or that androgeny would be ideal because it negates my femininity and really I'm learning to love my body **BUT** I don't want to be a victim of my biology either **BUT** I enjoy being a mother **BUT** I hate the guilt **BUT** I'm working on guilt **BUT** then I get guilty about not being guilty **BUT** I do want to have meaningful work besides being a mother **BUT** right now I have to do the laundry **BUT** if you want to know more about women's **BUTS** talk to any of my friends because I've decided no more **BUTS** . . . but . . . .

Random Moments

In the singles bar
The men come and go
With dreams
of being
A gigolo.

*   *   *

In the washroom
Women spritz their hair
And rearrange
Their underwear

*   *   *

In the suburbs
Couples fight
Then make up
Make love all night

*   *   *

In the schoolyard
Children play
And dream of growing up
Someday

*   *   *

In the churches
People pray
That God lives on
And life's okay

*   *   *

In my bedroom
Late at night
I cry sometimes
And hold on tight

*   *   *

In my kitchen
When it's sunny
I mostly think
That life is funny

*   *   *

And when I'm dead
I'll question God
Why all my life
Life seemed so odd

*   *   *

Then I will search
For William Blake
And ask him out
For mocha cake

Ever-Spinning Cupid

Cupid
(spinning
red cardboard cut-out silhouette
twirling by a thread from his head
above a chocolate box display
at Shoppers Drug Mart)
is taking aim again

I dart down
the shampoo and conditioner aisle
peek back out

and there he is again
cherub baby innocent
with his evil grin

you'll never get away
you'll never get away

I can yes I can
I can
I'm the gingerbread man

Shoppers look up momentarily from
their study of the shelves: cough drops nasal spray
lotions creams and jellies
condoms diapers toenail clippers vitamins

I escape down the beauty product aisle
stopping to buy some bubble bath
and candles
take the bus back home

Cupid has followed
sits down beside me

I give up
You win

I surrender
once again
knowing
I will always
choose
to be Cupid's willing victim
just because

Whatever poison lingers in my veins
from the arrows of Eros
will not cause my death
as quickly as a sterile life in which

I feign amnesia
forget that love
is the prescription
most of us came here for
in the first place

Diana's circus

Interior Decorating

It happened gradually.

First,
Diana papered her walls
in red-and-white-striped canvas
stuck a blue flag
in the chimney

no one seemed to notice
when her house became a tent
when her daily schedule
started to include
lion-taming
sword-swallowing
if they noticed
it didn't matter anyhow

so they would leave
for aerobics class
without her
after a while
stopped inviting her
to Tupperware parties

Diana! She'll be too busy
don't bother to even ask
this week, I think she's
training seals.

Diana happily went about
the study of her circus art
pleased that no one knew
the zoning bylaw
no circuses allowed
in a residential area

it was difficult in winter
to keep the big top heated
but Diana, holding a magnifying glass
up to the moon
managed to stay warm

by spring
she had perfected many tricks
sometimes moved the circus
out of doors

Monday

After supper, having cleared
the table, she retreats
to the kitchen
pretends to do the dishes

really, she practises her
plate-spinning act
using mop and broom handles
Royal Doulton china plates
from her wedding set

she imagines
each plate
is a person
or a thing
more precious than the cost
of the china

plate one is her husband
plates two and three are her children
plate four is her lover

this way there is an urgency
that makes her pay attention
and improves her timing

wetting her finger she begins with
plate number one
then races across
the kitchen
down the line
until she gets them all going

she hears applause
she is on Ed Sullivan
sighs of admiration
intake of breath
as the plates begin to wobble
slow down
start to crash

she has broken many plates
there are only these four left
but she hasn't missed once
in over a month of Mondays

Tuesday

Diana is the props person
the rock painter
she paints the rocks
on her front lawn
white
yes, just give Diana
a bucket of whitewash
she's delirious
with happiness

she would whitewash the world
if she could
make everything
clean
clean
clean
clean

sparkle polish buff shine
rinse her brush with turpentine
and look:

white and bright and new again

rub-a-dub-dub
three men in my tub

Mr. Clean you old bald-headed gypsy you devil you
Man from Glad
the incredible gift
of your green garbage
bags
Mr. Muscle
how grimy my life would be
without you

dustballs
minuscule molecules
of lint
   fluff
   fur
   hair
would grow to snowball size
attract rats cockroaches ants
leading to an overwhelming question
and death
ultimately death
for all who live here

mop broom vacuum cleaner
assemble
toilet bowl
surrender

hang out the sheets
worn in, worn out
the wash and rinse
of many cycles

froth over
frost over
the cake
which tastes almost as good
as homemade
home-aid
cleaning aids
Band-Aids

to live in a house that looks like the house that looks like the
house that looks like the house that looks like the house

beside it

to look through the world through sheers
from Simpsons Sears
to sit on the sofa sipping tea
to embrace the birch tree
to caress that tree with eyes
that travel up and out
to the farthest branch
to weep about that smallest
twig that touches sky
the world is happening out there
up there
way beyond   above my grasp

On Tuesday, Diana
paints the rocks on her front lawn
part of the job of the props person
is to make sure the entrance to the circus
is clearly marked

Wednesday

In the morning,
Diana trains the dog
to leap through
her daughter's hula hoop
rewards him
with a milkbone

she plays the radio
on stereo f.m.
there is a connection
between dog training
and classical music

the dog responds best to:
guitar
cello
harpsichord

After lunch,
Diana takes a scrub bucket
goes into the woods
in search of bears

she wants to teach the bears
to dance
she turns the bucket upside down
sits
waits

there are never any bears
but the raccoons are regulars
Diana lifts them
onto bucket-base
coaches them
in hind-leg waltz

but it is only a minor triumph

Diana would have preferred
the honesty of bears
who do not hide behind masks
who let you see their teeth
from the beginning

Thursday

Diana lets herself
be led
to the basement door

lets herself be tied there
the meter man comes in

he is the knife-thrower
he has stabbed her only once
but it wasn't a mistake
he only misses when he wants to

he's that good

Diana admits this is her least favourite trick
in fact she is thinking of cancelling this act
much better to work solo

all the same
she will miss the cigarette they share
after the performance

Friday

Diana has taken a swing
from the children's playset

suspended it
from a tree branch
in the yard

she shinnies up
a rope
climbs
to the treehouse
platform

then she begins her act
on the swinging trapeze

she used to perform in a leotard
but this caused
the neighbours some concern

her buttocks show
she doesn't shave
down there

the children should not see so much

so last Friday, Diana
went swinging in the trees naked

no one noticed

soon she will have to start charging admission

Saturday

o clown diana who juggles the moon and bananas and
cabbages too the eggs in the baskets she spits from her mouth
egg juggler her mouth has so much blowing power o clown
Diana who is known to take blue penis-shaped balloons and
twist them squeaking into french poodles and pass them out
to children all clustered like jellybeans in her backyard her
wig is really popcorn and her red nose a tomato she grew
in her garden o diana we won't laugh for you o clown who
tumbles her clothes in the dryer and practises somersaults
and flips

Sunday

On Sunday morning Diana practises tight-rope walking
barefoot on her clothesline. The first morning she did this
her washing machine ceased.

— she sure knows how to hang a good line —

That is what they used to say about Diana before that
morning. Now the children watch from windows. The
shutters flutter like eyelashes. The other mothers pretend not
to notice but silently applaud Diana's sense of balance.

— it isn't very high and besides, I don't mind a few broken bones
while I'm learning

Night Shift

Sometimes at night
you can hear Diana
with a hammer
in the basement
working by moonlight
she is creating
a merry-go-round
that will run on
dish detergent
make bubbles as it spins
around
and up
a spiral
pointing to the stars
playing a tune
that sounds like flutes
tin whistles
the horses will be unicorns
and wear roses
in their bridles
and when it is done
she will take a megaphone
invite everyone to
come to
Diana's circus

Postscript

For over a year
Diana held her circus
worked late nights
on the never-ending
merry-go-round
construction
kept the flag flying
she even inserted a ruby
in her navel
learned to ride
on elephants
she passed out tickets

no one ever came

just watched silently
from behind curtains

So Diana decided
to take the ultimate risk
to walk the clothesline tightrope
barefoot
blindfolded

She practised after dark

One morning Diana was found
wrapped around
the line
the way a bedspread
blown by wind
can tangle up inside itself

— she must have lost her balance
— we will miss Diana and her circus

the other women remembered
to only walk the clothesline tightrope
barefoot

when the sun was out
when the wind was just a breeze
when there was no danger
of being
knocked off balance

but Diana's story is not over

truth is, Diana left
stuffed pillows on that clothesline
she ran away from her circus
taking her merry-go-round along
as planned

I helped her escape

she lives where she must
on the moon of course
she keeps meaning to send me a postcard
but happiness makes her forgetful

up there where there are no laws of gravity
Diana free-forms
performs
old tricks
the merry-go-round makes
dish soap bubbles
that float alongside the stars
and the angels